LIFE LESSONS

for

LITTLE

LEARNERS

LOUISE MASON AND JANINE MOTLEY

LIFE LESSONS

for

LITTLE

LEARNERS

BEGINNING STEPS TOWARD ACADEMIC SUCCESS

TATE PUBLISHING
AND ENTERPRISES, LLC

This book is designed to provide accurate and authoritative information with regard to the subject matter covered. This information is given with the understanding that neither the author nor Tate Publishing, LLC is engaged in rendering legal, professional advice. Since the details of your situation are fact dependent, you should additionally seek the services of a competent professional.

The opinions expressed by the author are not necessarily those of Tate Publishing, LLC.

Published by Tate Publishing & Enterprises, LLC
127 E. Trade Center Terrace | Mustang, Oklahoma 73064 USA
1.888.361.9473 | www.tatepublishing.com

Tate Publishing is committed to excellence in the publishing industry. The company reflects the philosophy established by the founders, based on Psalm 68:11,
"The Lord gave the word and great was the company of those who published it."

Published in the United States of America

ISBN: 978-1-62510-760-2
1. Family & Relationships / Parenting / General
2. Family & Relationships / Parenting / Child Rearing
13.06.24

DEDICATION

To Brittish, Connor, and Kyra
Thanks for the laughs, love, and lessons
that inspired us to write this book.

ACKNOWLEDGEMENTS

We would like to express our gratitude to Gary and Connor and other family members who have supported and encouraged this book. We would also like to acknowledge the many students whose lives we have been privileged to touch.

CONTENTS

Introduction

The following stories, rhymes, and vignettes will expose your child to the ideas of *pride*, *dignity*, and *respect*. These three important qualities are learned from role models and personal experiences. Share with your children the idea that they should always be proud of who and what they are. Pride is developed through positive behavior and good choices in life. When children are proud of who and what they are, they will develop dignity. Dignity is that quality that helps develop a child's self-worth. Dignity will help your child to do his very best. Pride and dignity help to develop a healthy self-esteem. Respect is earned. When your child has mastered the art of etiquette, basic manners, treating others with respect, and being mindful of others' feelings, then he too can expect to be treated with common decency and respect.

Enjoy these stories with your children. Read and reread them together. You are giving them a great gift—a gift that will benefit them for the rest of their lives.

RESPECT FOR OTHERS

The following stories, rhymes, and vignettes will expose your child to the idea of respect. Respect is one of the most valuable tools that a child can possess. A child, whether he is two or twenty-two, should always respect his elders, his peers, and himself. It is through developing respect that your child will grow and mature to become that young adult you will be so proud of. When a child respects himself, he feels self worth; when a child respects others, he is generally respected in return.

Enjoy reading these stories to your children. They will emphasize the importance of respect both at home and at school.

ASKING PERMISSION AT HOME

Connor grabbed a cookie off the table. His mother saw him and raised her eyebrows and asked, "Connor, what do you say?"

Connor looked at his mom, smiled, and said, "Mother, may I? May I have a cookie?"

His mom smiled back and said, "May I have a cookie, what?"

Connor's eyes twinkled as he said, "May I have a cookie, please?"

His mom reached over the table, kissed his forehead, and gave Connor two more cookies. "Always remember, Connor, to be polite and to ask for permission," she said.

Connor smiled and said, "Thank you, Mom."

ASKING PERMISSION AT SCHOOL

The next day, while in school, Connor suddenly had to go to the bathroom. But his teacher was busy helping a little girl named Allison. Connor could not stand it anymore. He started dancing the bathroom jig! Connor looked at his teacher, started to interrupt her, then dashed to the door. He had just reached the door when he heard his teacher say, "Young man, where are you going?"

Connor turned around and said, "I'm going to the bathroom."

His teacher, Mrs. Peabody, walked over to Connor and said, "Remember, you must ask for permission before you leave the classroom."

"May I please use the bathroom, Mrs. Peabody?" Connor asked.

Mrs. Peabody smiled and said, "Of course you may."

Connor ran out the door. As he re-entered the classroom, Mrs. Peabody reminded him, "Never leave the classroom without permission from your teacher."

ASKING PERMISSION RHYME

Make sure to ask before you take or go.
The adult in charge always needs to know
What you are doing and where you are.
Just saying "Please" can take you far.

Disagreeing at Home

Connor and his little sister Kyra were arguing—again. He wanted to play with his toy trucks, and he wanted Kyra to play with him, but Kyra did not want to play with toy trucks. She wanted to run outside and play Hide n' Seek, and she wanted Connor to play with her. The two of them were yelling, very loudly at each other. Finally, their mom came over. She had listened to them long enough, hoping that they would be able to settle their differences. However, the arguing had continued. "What is wrong here?" she asked both of her children. "Do you feel that this arguing will get you anywhere?" she asked. "Compromise," she said.

"What is that?" asked the ever curious Kyra.

"I know," Connor said. "Compromise is when we both agree to give in a little bit, but somehow get what we both want. Isn't that right, Mom?" asked Connor.

Mom smiled. "Yes," she said, "that is exactly what a compromise is. Now, how can the two of you agree to play together and both get what you want?"

Connor and Kyra looked at each other suspiciously. "Hmm…" Kyra said. "I know," she said excitedly. "Connor, why don't we play hide-and-seek, then when we get tired of running around, we can play with your trucks."

Connor looked at his sister. He did want to play with his trucks; however, he figured if she was willing to do both, then so was he. "Okay," Connor said, "hide-and-seek first, then trucks." Kyra and Connor looked at their mom. She was smiling at her two children who had come to an agreement.

"Go play," she said, "and have fun."

DISAGREEING AT SCHOOL

Two days later, Kyra was at recess. She looked around. The playground was filled with exciting equipment to play on. There were red and green teeter-totters to share with a friend, swings to take her high into the sky as though she was flying with the birds, and a merry-go-round to spin on until she was dizzy with laughter.

Kyra just could not make up her mind where she wanted to go. She saw her friends Caleb and William on the teeter-totter; Mackenzie and Mallory were swinging on the swings, and three or four of her other friends were laughing on the merry-go-round.

"C'mon," Mallory invited Kyra, "come on and swing with us."

Kyra looked around the playground. What she really wanted to do, she decided, was to play on the teeter-totter with her best friend, Caleb. But Caleb was still on the teeter-totter with William!

Kyra said, "No, thanks" to Mallory and ran over to the teeter-totter. "Get off," she demanded to William. "I want to play with Caleb now."

William was surprised at Kyra's tone of voice. "You can't tell me what to do," he shouted at her from his lofty perch high in the sky.

Kyra stamped her foot and crossed her arms across her chest. She wanted to play with Caleb.

Mrs. Dunmuffin, the recess supervisor, said to Kyra, "Kyra, you cannot demand someone to do something just because you want your own way. You have to ask nicely and wait for your turn."

Kyra remembered what her brother had taught her the other day about compromise, something about everybody giving in a little bit to get what they wanted. "I am sorry, Mrs. Dunmuffin," Kyra said. "Hey, William, do you think you can play with Caleb just a little bit more, and then I can ride the teeter-totter with him?" Kyra smiled and looked hopefully at William.

"Sure," William said, "I will be off in just a few more minutes."

Kyra, William, and Caleb all looked at Mrs. Dunmuffin for approval. She nodded and smiled at them and said, "Now that's the way you should always speak to each other."

DISAGREE RHYME

We may not always get along and agree,
But if we talk calmly and share, we can see.
A way to work together and all live happily.

VOICE LEVELS AT HOME

Kyra and Connor were arguing—again. Their voices were getting louder and louder. Their dad came in and said, "What is going on in here? You know your mother worked late last night and is trying to sleep."

Connor looked at his dad and said, "Dad, it's Kyra. She's trying to pull the cat's tail, and I keep telling her that that is not a nice thing to do."

Dad raised his eyebrows as he looked at his daughter. "Honey, is that true?"

Kyra giggled and smiled impishly at her dad.

"Daddy, I just want to hear Shadow talk," she said as she tilted her head to the side and smiled up at her dad.

"Two things," their dad said. "One, Kyra, you may not pull the cat's tail because if he talks, it is because you are hurting him. And two, you are both going to wake up your mother with your loud voices. Please go outside and play."

Connor and Kyra looked at each other. "Okay, Dad," they said, "we promise to use inside voices inside, and we will go outside and play."

Then Kyra looked at her dad and said, "I promise not to pull Shadow's tail anymore. Love you, daddy," she whispered with her extra-quiet inside voice and she ran outside to play with her brother.

Voice Levels at School

Several days later, Connor was in math class. Today, they were studying multiplications. Connor enjoyed math, especially when they were doing group work. Today, his teacher, Mr. Cornberry, had allowed them to choose their own groups. Now that was Connor's favorite time for math. Connor grouped up with his three best friends, Stephen, Jalen, and Bobby.

Mr. Cornberry explained the students' group work then said, "Now remember, class, you must keep your voices low so that the other groups can hear each other."

At first, Connor's group kept their voices low. Then as the time went on, they became more animated in their discussion. Their voices became louder and louder. At one point, they heard an *uh-um* from their teacher. The boys looked up and saw Mr. Cornberry looking at them with "the look" on his face.

"Shh…" Connor said. The group immediately lowered their voices.

Five minutes later, Connor's group became loud again.

"Gentlemen," Mr. Cornberry said, "I have already given you a verbal and a nonverbal warning. Since you choose to disobey me, you must finish the work on your own. No more help from each other."

The boys looked at each and sighed. "This is not fair," Stephen muttered under his breath.

Connor thought about the conversation he had with his dad several days ago. His dad had talked to him about inside voices. He looked at his friends and said, "Hey you guys, we were warned to keep our voices down. We didn't listen. Next time, we will just speak softer."

VOICE LEVELS RHYME

When you have something to say,
Don't just yell out, "Mom!" "Dad!" "Teacher! Hey!"
Wait quietly or raise your hand;
And they will get to you as soon as they can.

SHARING AT HOME

"It's mine."

"No, it's mine."

"No, I said it was mine, and anyway, I had it first."

The voices were getting louder and louder from the other room. Unable to take anymore, Mom walked in and took the toy that they were arguing over away from her two children, Kyra and Connor. "Now, it is mine," she said. "If the two of you cannot share, then nobody gets to play with it." Mom walked back into the other room with the much-prized toy.

"Now do you see what you did?" Connor asked his sister. "Now neither one of us gets to play with it." Kyra stuck her lip out, crossed her arms and pouted. "It's your fault, "she muttered crossly. "I had it first."

For the next few minutes, Kyra and Connor just glared at each other. Finally, Connor said, "Okay, how about if you play with it first, then I get to play with it after you are finished?"

Kyra looked at him suspiciously. "Why are you being so nice?" she asked.

Connor looked at his sister and sighed. "Geez, can't I do anything nice without you getting suspicious? I just want to play with it. I know," he said thoughtfully, "how about if you and I play together? Mom would like that. She's always telling us to share our toys and learn how to play together without arguing."

Kyra thought about what her brother had just said. Their mom was always telling them to play nice. "Okay," she said. "Let's go ask Mom if we can have the toy back."

Mom was listening to her children's discussion. She was hoping that they would come to a solution. As Kyra and Connor entered the kitchen, she turned to them and smiled. "Yes?" she asked them. "Is there something I can do for you?"

"May we have the toy back?" Connor asked. "We thought it would be better to play with it together than not be able to play with it at all."

Their mother smiled. "Yes," she said. "It is better to share than not to have anything at all. I am very proud of you both."

Kyra and Connor smiled at their mom then at each other. It was much more fun to play together than to argue.

SHARING AT SCHOOL

Several days later Kyra was sitting in the school cafeteria with her friends. They were just getting ready to open their lunches and eat. Kyra opened her bag and smiled. Her dad had packed her two peanut butter and jelly sandwiches, a bag of potato chips, a tube of yogurt, and a Juicy Juice.

Kyra and her friends looked around at each other's lunches. They loved to trade their food. As Kyra looked around, she saw a new student sitting by herself with no lunch.

"Come over here and sit with us," Kyra said to the new girl.

The new girl came over and joined Kyra and her friends. "What's your name?" Kyra asked.

"My name is Angie," the new girl said. "What's yours?"

"My name is Kyra. Where's your lunch?" Kyra asked her.

"We didn't have anything to eat," Angie said. "So I didn't bring anything."

Kyra looked at the food her dad had packed. She looked at her friends. "Hey, you guys," Kyra said to her friends, "do you think we can give Angie some of our food to eat?"

All of the girls shared their food with Angie. She smiled at them and said, "Thank you, guys. This really makes me feel good."

All of the girls smiled, and Kyra felt really good about sharing.

SHARING RHYME

I give to you; you give to me.
Then you and me become a we.
So there's no reason to scream and shout
'Cause that's not what sharing is all about.

INTERRUPTING AT HOME

One day, Kyra's grandma was talking to her neighbor, Mrs. Duff, but Kyra wanted to ask her grandma a question. Kyra reached up and tugged at her grandma's shirttail. "Grandma," Kyra said demandingly.

Her grandma, however, kept right on talking.

"Grandma!" she said again, louder this time.

Her grandma reached down and removed Kyra's fingers from her shirt, but she did not acknowledge Kyra.

Again, Kyra reached up and tugged at her grandma's shirt. "Grandma, listen to me," Kyra said.

Finally, Grandma said, "Excuse me, Mrs. Duff." Then she looked down and said, "Kyra, stop interrupting. It is not polite to interrupt people when they are speaking."

"But I have a question," Kyra tried to explain.

"You will have to be patient and wait," her grandma said. "Then it will be your turn to have all my attention."

INTERRUPTING LEARNING
PROCESS AT SCHOOL

Connor was always acting silly in school. He loved having the other boys' and girls' attention. He loved having the teacher's attention too. What he enjoyed most was making everybody laugh. He spoke out loud. He interrupted others, and he was always getting out of his seat without the teacher's permission.

His classmates thought he was funny at first, but then bad things started to happen. The boys and girls became mad at him because they could not hear the teacher. His teacher became upset with him too. Nobody would laugh with him. Then they all started to ignore him. They even stopped playing with him. Nobody wanted to be his friend.

So Connor sat by himself and thought and thought and thought. He did not like being the class clown. He did not like missing what the teacher was saying during class, so he started to put his hand up when he had a question or something to say. He stopped saying silly and funny things and standing up when the teacher was speaking.

Then good things started to happen. The teacher smiled at him when he raised his hand before he spoke. The other students listened to what he had to say. He became friends again with his classmates. They started to play with him again. Connor was happy and learning more, and the other students were learning more too.

INTERRUPTING LEARNING PROCESS RHYME

Put your hand up or say "Excuse me," before you shout.
This is what good manners are all about.

List and discuss with your child other ways of showing respect. Write them here and review them together.

_____

_____

_____

_____

_____

_____

_____

_____

_____

_____

_____

_____

_____

_____

RESPONSIBILITY

The following stories, rhymes, and vignettes will teach your child the importance of responsibility. In order to be truly successful in school and in life, a child must learn to be responsible. A responsible person takes care of what needs to be done without being told. He takes the initiative and sees a task to completion. He becomes, therefore, someone who is reliable and trustworthy.

Learning responsibility starts at home. Share these stories with your children. Assign them responsibilities in the home. This will encourage them to have a good sense of responsibility in all facets of their lives.

PICKING UP AFTER ONE'S SELF AT HOME

Kyra was playing with her building blocks all morning. She loved to put the same colored blocks together. She loved to build houses, roads, and huge towers. Then, she loved to knock them down and watch the colorful blocks fly in every direction. Soon, it was time for lunch.

Her dad called her into the kitchen. "Kyra, time for lunch. Let's go."

"Coming, Dad," Kyra called. Kyra ran into the kitchen, ate her lunch, and ran outside to play.

Her dad walked into the living room and gave a big sigh. He saw Kyra's blocks all over the room. They were under the table, on top of the chairs, and all over the floor. "Kyra," her dad went over to the window and called her name. "Please come back in here."

Kyra came running into the house. She looked at her dad. He did not look happy. "Kyra, what are the rules about picking up after one's self?" he asked her.

Kyra looked at all the blocks in the living room. She did not like to pick up her toys when she was done playing. She tapped her foot on the floor but did not answer.

"Kyra?" her dad asked again. "I'm waiting."

Kyra took a deep breath. "I don't like to pick up the blocks," she said. "It takes too much time."

Her dad looked at her quietly. He thought for a moment. "Kyra," he said. "What would our house look like if no one picked up after themselves? There would be things everywhere on the floor, and soon, we would not be able to move around. You would end up sitting on your blocks and tripping over your toys. Then you wouldn't be able to find anything."

Kyra thought about that. "You're right," she said.

"So," her dad said. "What's the rule?"

"I know. I have to pick up my toys when I am done playing with them," she said.

"That's right," her dad replied. "Remember, there is a place for everything and everything in its place."

PICKING UP AFTER ONE'S SELF IN SCHOOL

Play time! It was Kyra's favorite time at school. She and her friends could choose to play with any toy in the play area. Kyra and her friends loved to color and make pictures. Then they could cut out their pictures and paste them on the colorful boards.

Play time was almost over. Their teacher, Ms. Dino, told them to pick up their toys and put everything away.

Kyra began picking up the colored markers and putting them in their boxes. Her friends, however, ran away and did not help her.

"Hey, you guys," Kyra said. "Ms. Dino told us we had to pick up our toys."

LOUISE MASON AND JANINE MOTLEY

Her friends just shrugged their shoulders and did not listen to Kyra.

"Hey!" Kyra said again, louder this time. Ms. Dino heard Kyra calling for her friends to help.

"Girls," Ms. Dino said, "what should you be doing right now?"

Kyra's friends all looked at each other and walked back to the play area.

Ms. Dino said, "Everybody helps and the job will get done quicker that way."

"Okay, Ms. Dino," the girls said. They ran over to Kyra and started to help put things away. Very quickly, the job was done.

"Good job, girls," Ms. Dino said. "Let's get back to our reading."

The friends all smiled at each other and ran back to their desks.

PICKING UP AFTER ONE'S SELF RHYME

Everyone has a job to do,
Remember, everyone is counting on you,
Be responsible; get your job done,
Doing your part helps everyone.

Helping Clean Up Messes at Home

One bright summer day, Kyra and her friends were outside playing ball, blowing and popping bubbles, and lying on the ground discovering pictures in the clouds when her mother called, "Kyra, come in. It's time for lunch."

Kyra wanted to get back to playing as soon as possible, so she ran into the house, up the stairs, and into the bathroom to wash her hands. In fact, she was in such a hurry she accidentally knocked over a bottle of shampoo. Down went the bottle, and shampoo oozed down the side of the sink and slithered onto the floor.

"Oh no," Kyra said to herself, but she did not want to take the time to clean up, so she ran downstairs, quickly ate her lunch, and hurried back outside to play.

It was not long, however, before she heard her mother calling her in a voice that told Kyra her mom had discovered the slippery, soapy mess.

"*Kyra Leigh*, get in here right now, and clean up the mess you made," her mother demanded.

As they worked together to clean up the mess, Kyra apologized to her mother and thanked her for helping her wipe the sticky, slimy shampoo off the sink and floor.

When they had finished, her mom explained, "Even though I accept your apology, there are always consequences for the choices we make. Because you did not tell me about the spilled shampoo, you may not go back outside to play."

Kyra felt sad, but she knew she had learned some good lessons that day. She had learned to take her time, to tell an adult if an accident happens, and that it is better to lose a little playtime instead of a lot.

HELPING TO CLEAN UP
MESSES AT SCHOOL

Kyra's favorite part of preschool was the time Ms. Silver called art. During art, all kinds of colorful materials to make fun things like masks and finger paints were placed on the table. The only part about art time Kyra did not much care for was the clean up afterward.

Today, for example, Kyra was a little tired, so when Ms. Silver announced, "Time to clean up," Kyra just put her head down on the table.

"Kyra," Joey, one of her classmates, said, "you have to help too."

"I'm too tired," Kyra told Joey.

Ms. Silver heard them talking, and she told Kyra, "We must all be responsible and clean up after ourselves so our classroom will be nice for us all."

Kyra then remembered that at home everyone had to do their part, so she knew she also needed to help at school.

When all the art supplies were neatly put away, Ms. Silver said, "Thank you, class, for doing such a fine job."

Everyone felt proud, and Kyra was especially glad she had helped too.

HELPING CLEAN UP MESSES RHYME

When there is something to be done,
Working may not seem like much fun,
But if everyone lends a hand to do it,
It's amazing how fast you'll zip right through it.

DOING CHORES AT HOME

One day, Kyra and her mom went to visit Kate and Caleb and their mom, Mrs. Winston. As they entered the house, however, Kyra's mom tripped over a big red toy fire engine and almost fell. As Kyra looked around, she saw that toys were everywhere except in the empty toy box where they belonged. There were also clothes scattered on the floor, and when they went into the bright, sunny kitchen, Kyra noticed dirty dishes piled high in the sink.

Later that afternoon when she and her mom returned home, Kyra went to her room to play. She quickly realized, however, that many of her toys were not where they belonged.

Recalling the incident when her mom tripped, Kyra decided she needed to do a better job of keeping her room neat and safe. She carefully put all her toys where they belonged.

As she looked around her room, Kyra felt proud of what she had done. Nobody would trip over toys in her room.

DOING CHORES AT SCHOOL

At Bright Eyes Preschool, the students in Mrs. Snicker's class took turns doing weekly duties. For example, this week, Terrence was to clean the board and Julie was to check to see that the boxes of art supplies were put away properly.

Kyra, however, had one of the most important jobs of all. She was to flip the calendar to show the day and date when she came in every morning so everyone would know what day of the month it was.

Today, however, Kyra had forgotten. She and her friend, Caleb, had been talking and laughing so much that morning that she forgot. When Mrs. Snickers said, "Good morning, class, and how is everyone on this fine day of…" She pointed to the calendar as she always did so that the class could say the date together, but instead, everyone started to giggle.

It was then that Kyra remembered. She had forgotten to flip the calendar when she came in, so it still showed yesterday's date. Mrs. Snickers quickly quieted the class and asked Kyra to change the date.

That was a day Kyra would never forget. That day, she learned more than just school lessons. She learned, just like at home, everyone has to do the jobs they are given in order to make the day run smoothly.

DOING CHORES RHYME

When you are given a job to do,
It's really not a job just for you.
It's to help get everything done better;
Doing your part helps it all come together.

Developing Independence at Home

Doing her own chores on Saturdays and helping everyday by putting her things where they belonged, made Kyra feel like a big person. She felt big like Dad, Mom, and Connor, instead of like a baby.

Now Dad, Mom, and Connor allowed her to help with things they told her she was too little to do before. Mom let her do special jobs like tear the lettuce for salads, take the hair off the corn on the cob, and help set the table. She and Dad had fun spraying each other with water when she helped him wash the car, and Connor even allowed her to go into his bedroom to play *Sesame Street* games on his computer.

Kyra liked being trusted by her brother, helping others, and doing more for herself. She could dress herself (even the clothes with buttons and zippers), eat without making too much of a mess, and go to the bathroom all alone.

Kyra did not like being treated like a baby. She loved babies, but babies needed help to do everything. Now that she was able to do more on her own, Kyra felt like a big girl.

Developing Independence at School

Kyra loved preschool. She enjoyed learning wonderful new things in Mrs. Nightingale's class. There were always exciting stories from colorful books, great games, and fun projects to do.

The class usually worked together. That made learning even more fun. Today, however, Mrs. Nightingale did something different.

"Today," she explained, "you are going to work independently. This means each of you will work quietly by yourself without any help from your classmates. I will call out the letters of the alphabet, and you will color them in when you see them on your papers."

Mrs. Nightingale then passed out the papers and colored pencils. The students were very quiet as she began calling out the letters.

Kyra listened carefully and colored each letter as it was called. To her surprise, as she colored, a picture began to appear.

When Mrs. Nightingale stopped calling out letters, she said, "If you can see the picture of a dinosaur, you have colored all the letters correctly."

Kyra was delighted. Her dinosaur was colorful and clear, and she was especially proud because she had done it all by herself.

DEVELOPING INDEPENDENCE RHYME

Babies are cute.
Babies are fun,
But you don't always want to be treated like one.
Big girls and big boys are what you want to become,
But to be treated like a big person, you must act like one.

List and discuss with your child other ways of showing responsibility. Write them here and review them together.

_____

_____

_____

_____

_____

_____

_____

_____

_____

_____

_____

_____

_____

_____

_____

ACCOUNTABILITY

The following stories, rhymes, and vignettes will teach your child the importance of accountability. When a child learns to be accountable for his actions, he will give more careful thought and consideration to his choices and conduct. He will become, therefore, a more responsible individual. It is also through accountability that a child realizes what he is capable of. If a child learns at an early age that he must be responsible and accountable for his choices, he is more likely to proceed in life with an open mind and a sense of responsibility for his own academic success.

Read these stories to your children with the understanding that they must be accountable for their own actions.

TELLING THE TRUTH &
UNDERSTANDING
CONSEQUENCES AT HOME

Kyra's grandma was in the kitchen when she heard a loud noise. *Crack!* Just then, Kyra came running out of her grandma's bedroom, her eyes wide with fright.

"Kyra," her grandmother said, "what happened?"

Kyra, who knew she was not supposed to touch things in her grandma's bedroom without permission, said, "Nothing, Mi Ma," using her pet name for her grandma.

"Kyra, are you telling me the truth?" her grandma asked.

Kyra did not respond. She knew that she had done wrong. She had picked up her grandmother's favorite glass elephant. Unfortunately, the elephant had slipped out of her hands while she was holding it.

Kyra was frightened. She knew she was in trouble. Should she lie and tell her Mi Ma she didn't do anything, or should she tell her the truth that she had disobeyed her by not following the rules?

Kyra gave a big sigh. She knew what she had to do. Her mother had always told her to tell the truth. Nothing was worse than lying. Lying would result in double trouble; she would be in trouble for disobeying *and* for lying.

Kyra hung her head in shame. She knew that she had done wrong. Better to own up to her actions. "I'm sorry, Mi Ma," she said. "I went into your bedroom without permission. All I wanted to do was to touch your beautiful glass elephant."

"What happened in my bedroom?" Kyra's grandmother asked her.

"I dropped your elephant, and it broke," Kyra said.

Now it was grandma's turn to give a big sigh. "Kyra," she said, "that was my oldest and favorite elephant. Now it is broken all because you did not follow the rules." Kyra's grandma gave another sigh. "You know that there will be a consequence for your behavior."

"Yes, Mi Ma, I know," Kyra replied. "And I promise I won't touch things in your bedroom without permission ever again."

"Thank you, Kyra," her grandmother said. "Thank you also for telling the truth and for being responsible for your actions."

TELLING THE TRUTH & UNDERSTANDING CONSEQUENCES AT SCHOOL

Today was the day of Connor's big spelling test. He had been studying for this test for several days. He knew how to spell every word and knew their definitions. In spelling class, Connor sat next to James. Before class started, Connor and James were quizzing each other about their words.

Mr. Crabapple called the class to order. "Okay, students, everything off your desks. Be quiet. You know the rules when taking a test—absolutely no talking and no looking at your neighbor's paper."

After the test, the students went out for recess. "Geez," Connor said, "that test was just a little more difficult than I thought it would be. But I think I did okay on it. How about you, James? How do you think you did?"

James hung his head and said, "I think I did okay, Connor."

The next day, after class, Mr. Crabapple told Connor and James he wanted to speak to them. Connor looked at James with a questioning look on his face. James just shrugged his shoulders, and the two boys approached Mr. Crabapple's desk.

"Well, boys," Mr. Crabapple said, "is there something either one of you wants to tell me?"

Connor looked perplexed. James, once again, hung his head. Connor said, "Mr. Crabapple, I'm not sure what you are asking."

Mr. Crabapple looked at both Connor and James and then placed both of their vocabulary tests on his desk for the boys to look at. Connor and James looked. Both boys had misspelled the same words. However, not only did they misspell the same words, they spelled them incorrectly in exactly the same way!

Mr. Crabapple watched the two boys. He knew one of them had cheated; he just didn't know which one. He waited for them to tell him the truth. "Well?" Mr. Crabapple said. "I'm waiting. If one of you does not tell me you cheated, you both fail the test, and I will contact both of your parents."

Connor looked over at James. Connor knew that he did not cheat on his test. "James?" Connor asked.

James looked down at the floor. He started to fidget. "I cheated off of Connor," James said. "He had no idea that I was looking at his paper."

Connor looked at James in surprise. This was his friend. He was thankful that James had told the truth, but he was also sad that James had cheated.

Mr. Crabapple looked at both boys. "James," he said, "thank you for being honest. If you spend more time studying and getting to know the material, you will not have to cheat on your test. Cheating will get you nowhere in life."

"I am sorry, Mr. Crabapple," James said. "It will not happen again. Do you have to call my parents?" he asked remorsefully.

"Yes, James, I do," Mr. Crabapple said. "Now before you leave the room, is there something you wanted to say to Connor as well?"

"Sorry, Connor," James said. He was embarrassed. He knew he was wrong to cheat off of his friend's test.

"Thanks, James," Connor said. "The next time we have a test, we'll just have to make sure we study together so we both know the material. Okay?"

"Okay," James said.

They walked out of the room smiling at each other.

TELLING THE TRUTH & UNDERSTANDING CONSEQUENCES RHYME

Always avoid telling a lie.
It's too much work to try and try
To keep it secret and be sly.
So tell the truth even when you're wrong.
There will be consequences, but they won't last long.

List and discuss with your child other ways of showing accountability. Write them here and review them together.

_____

_____

_____

_____

_____

_____

_____

_____

_____

_____

_____

_____

_____

_____

_____

_____

LOVE OF LEARNING

The following stories, rhymes, and vignettes will teach your child the importance of developing a love of learning. Your child has so much to learn to become a responsible young adult. You want your child to appreciate a good education and to understand that learning will take place for the rest of his life. A child must understand that in order to be successful, he must learn; learning gives a sense of accomplishment, and accomplishment gives a sense of pride.

Enjoy reading these stories to your children. But most importantly, teach your child to have an open mind and to learn everything he can. Learning will take him anywhere he wants to go.

You want your child to be prepared for his social and academic future. You want him to embrace the concept that learning is what matters. Learning will make him feel better about himself. You can make this possible by working with him and preparing him for his social and academic future.

READING TOGETHER AT HOME

"Okay, Connor," his dad called out. "It's reading time."

Connor yelled back, "Dad, I don't want to read tonight. Please don't make me." Connor was busy playing with his computer games, and he did not want to stop to read any boring old books.

"Connor," his dad said, "what is the rule?"

"I know, Dad," Connor said. "I need to read for thirty minutes every day. But, Dad, could you read with me tonight?"

"What do you mean, Connor? How can I read with you?" his dad asked.

"You know, maybe if you read a paragraph and then I can read one? Or maybe you can be one character and I can be the other? What do you think, Dad?" Connor asked his dad hopefully. "Will you read with me?"

His dad looked at Connor's big blue eyes wide with anticipation. "Of course I will son," his dad replied. "Reading can be something special we can do together."

"Aw gee, thanks, Dad," Connor said as he reached out to hug his father.

READING TOGETHER AT SCHOOL

Kyra was shy and quiet. She did not say very much in school. She did not like to hear her voice. As a result, she had trouble reading out loud. She did not like other students listening to her. Sometimes she mispronounced a word, and some of the kids would laugh. They would laugh softly, but she knew that they were laughing at her.

Kyra had a best friend named Devon. Devon knew that Kyra was afraid to read out loud. He wanted to do something for Kyra to help her. He knew that if she believed in herself, she wouldn't mind reading out loud. He had an idea.

"Mrs. Peabody," Devon said. "I have an idea that may help Kyra get over her fear of reading out loud."

Mrs. Peabody looked at Devon with her kind big brown eyes. She knew that Devon really wanted to help his friend.

"What is your idea?" she asked Devon.

"Well," Devon said, "how about if we read in pairs? That way, whenever Kyra has to read out loud, I can read with her. Then she will get used to the sound of her voice in the classroom."

Mrs. Peabody smiled at Devon. "That," she said, "is a really wonderful idea. We will try it."

The next day, Mrs. Peabody told her students to get into their reading circle. After taking her place in the circle, Kyra tried to hide behind her book, hoping that Mrs. Peabody would not notice her and call on her to read.

"Next up for reading will be…Kyra and Devon," Mrs. Peabody said.

Kyra looked around surprised, "Devon will read with me?" she asked.

"Yes, Kyra," Mrs. Peabody said. "Devon will read with you."

Kyra smiled shyly at Devon. He smiled back, and together they began to read.

READING TOGETHER RHYME

ABC's are only letters;
That is until they come together.
Words make stories exciting and fun,
So reading is great for everyone.

MAKING LEARNING FUN AT HOME

"C'mon, Kyra. Time to review your numbers," Connor said.

Kyra looked at her big brother and frowned. "You are not my dad, and you cannot make me work on my numbers," Kyra said.

Connor sighed. *Here we go again*, he thought.

Every night was the same old story. Connor, since he was the big brother, had the responsibility of reviewing numbers with her. The problem was that Kyra did not like reviewing her numbers. Connor thought of school. *What did his teachers do to make learning fun?* he wondered.

All of a sudden, Connor had an idea. "Hey, Mom," Connor said, "do we have any M&M's or other candy I can use to help Kyra enjoy learning her numbers?"

His mom looked at Connor and smiled, "Why, that is a wonderful idea," she said.

Connor walked into Kyra's bedroom with a smug smile on his face.

"What?" Kyra asked. "What are you thinking about with that smile?"

Connor just continued to smile and put down a plastic baggie filled with M&M's. "How about this?" Connor asked. "Every time you say the correct number, you can eat an M&M."

Kyra looked at her big brother and smiled. "Okay, now I am ready to learn. But only if you help me eat the M&M's," she said with a smile back at Connor.

"It's a deal," Connor said. "Let's learn and have some fun."

Making Learning Fun at School

Kyra and her friends were outside rolling around in the brightly colored leaves that had fallen to the ground. The leaves were everywhere. It was November, and Thanksgiving was just around the corner. The bell rang. The students returned to their seats; however, they did not settle down.

All of a sudden, Kyra heard "Gobble, Gobble." She and the other students immediately stopped their chatter and looked around surprised.

"Students," Ms. Freckles said, "it is almost Turkey Day. I am going to read you a story about the pilgrims, the Indians, and how Thanksgiving Day started."

While Ms. Freckles was reading the story and showing the pictures to the students, Kyra had an idea. "Ms. Freckles," Kyra said, "can we dress in those kinds of clothes? Can we pretend to be pilgrims and Indians?"

"What a great idea, Kyra," Ms. Freckles said. "Why don't we have our own Thanksgiving celebration? But," she continued, "we all have to share something we are thankful for."

The students were excited. "Hey," Kyra said, "how do we know if we are a pilgrim or an Indian?"

Ms. Freckles said, "We'll make this simple. This half of the room will be pilgrims, and this half of the room will be Indians."

The students could not stop talking about the pilgrims and Indians. As the end of the day neared, Ms. Freckles reminded them, "Don't forget," she said, "you can dress up next Thursday. And don't forget to talk to your parents about what you are thankful for."

By the time the final bell rang, the students were even more excited. They couldn't wait to go home and tell their parents that next Thursday they would be dressing up as pilgrims and Indians, sharing what they were thankful for, and eating pumpkin pie with whipped cream.

MAKING LEARNING FUN RHYME

Learning opens our minds to all that's new.
Whether learning reading, or writing,
or to add two plus two,
Learning can be exciting. It can even be fun.
Just add some creativity, and it won't be "Ho Hum."

MODELING LEARNING AT HOME

Connor's mom was doing laundry. She was folding clothes. Connor had watched his mom take clothes from the washer and put them in the dryer. Then he watched her take them from the dryer and place them into the laundry basket. His mom then took the basket into the bedroom and began folding clothes. Connor watched organization taking place out of the jumble of clothes in the basket. He saw how neat it looked. Everything was in its place.

Connor went into his bedroom. He picked up his pajamas from the floor. He also picked up his shirt and pants that were on the floor. He thought about his mom. He folded his pajamas. He folded his shirt and pants. Then he put everything away. Connor saw how neat it looked. He liked knowing that he could learn from his mom. Mom always made everything look organized.

MODELING LEARNING AT SCHOOL

At the end of every day, Connor listened to his teacher as she told the students to put things away. She would ask them to put their books in their desks, and she would also put her books in her desk. She would tell them to place their pencils in their pencil boxes, and she would put her pencils in her pencil box. The teacher, Mrs. Peabody, would request that they put their papers in their folders, and she would put her papers in her folder.

Connor was always amazed that his desk, which had been so messy, covered with books, papers, pencils, and other materials, would be neat, tidy, and organized at the end of the day. He felt good about organizing his things. Everything was in its place.

MODELING LEARNING RHYME

Teach me. Show me.
There's so much I want to know,
And watching you enjoy it too
Makes me want to learn more.

DEVELOPING FEELINGS OF ACCOMPLISHMENT AT HOME

"You did it!" Connor's mom said. "You did it, all by yourself. I am so proud of you," she said.

Connor looked down at the ground. "Mom," he said, "I could not have done it without your help. You taught me how to ride my bike. You ran beside me, keeping me straight so that I would not fall over."

Connor's mom looked at her son. She knew that her son had been afraid to ride his bike. He was afraid of falling down and getting hurt. All the boys in the neighborhood were beginning to tease and make fun of him because he had not yet learned how to ride his bike.

"Connor, I knew you could do it," his mom said. "All you needed was practice. You are the one who was determined to conquer your fear of falling."

Connor smiled at his mom. "Mom," he said, "I feel so good inside. I feel like I can do anything if I just try hard enough."

Connor's mom smiled back. "You are right," she said. "With determination and hard work, you can overcome all of your fears. You can accomplish almost anything."

DEVELOPING FEELINGS OF ACCOMPLISHMENT AT SCHOOL

Kyra had always been proud to tell people her name when she was asked. Today, however, she was no longer sure her name was great. The problem was, her teacher said she had to learn to *write* it! She had been trying and trying, but it still looked nothing like it was supposed to.

Connor walked into the kitchen and found his little sister, Kyra, at the table, writing on pieces of paper then tearing them up.

"I just can't do it," he heard her say.

"Can't do what?" Connor asked.

"I can't write my name," Kyra told Connor as big tears rolled down each cheek.

"Of course you can," Connor assured her.

"Just think of the letters as sticks. Watch. Make your *K* by first drawing a long stick. Then make two short sticks come out of the middle of that one, like this."

After watching Connor, Kyra tried. It worked.

"Now," Connor said, "draw a long slanted stick like this. Then make a short stick that slants away from the top of it like this."

Again Kyra followed Connor's directions. All of a sudden, a big smile began to cover her face. She was really writing her name.

"Okay," Connor went on, "the *r* is a little tricky, but it is not hard. Just draw a short stick like this, then make a short one that curves from the middle of it and out to the right."

Kyra made her *r* with no problem at all.

"The *a*," Connor told her, "is probably the easiest of all. Just draw a circle. Then draw a stick against the right side of it."

By the time Kyra finished writing her name, she was wearing the biggest smile ever.

"I did it, Connor!" she shouted! "I wrote my name! Thank you so much," she said, giving her big brother a huge hug.

"You're welcome," Connor said as he grabbed a shiny red apple out of the fruit bowl on the table and turned to leave the room. Then he quickly turned back around.

"One more thing," he said. "Don't ever say 'you can't.' If you try hard enough, you can do anything. Besides," he added with a sly grin, "you're my sister, so you have to be smart."

Kyra smiled back, made a promise to her brother never to give up on herself again, and continued to practice writing her name.

By the time she left the kitchen table, Kyra was proud to have the name *Kyra* again, and she could not wait to get back to school to show her teacher she could write it.

DEVELOPING FEELINGS OF ACCOMPLISHMENT RHYME

You did it, she cried
You did it because you tried.
Anything worth having is worth trying for.
And trying will only bring you more.

List and discuss with your child other ways of developing a love of learning. Write them here and review them together.

_____

_____

_____

_____

_____

_____

_____

_____

_____

_____

_____

_____

_____

_____

_____

_____